McLain Street Gang
Stories of My Hometown Newport, Arkansas

Rachel Shankles

McLain Street Gang
Copyright © 2018 by *Rachel Shankles.*

ISBN: 978-1-949231-32-8

All rights reserved.

No part of this publication may be reproduced, distributed, or transmitted in any form or by any means, including photocopying, recording, or other electronic or mechanical methods, without the prior written permission of the publisher, except in the case of brief quotations embodied in critical reviews and certain other noncommercial uses permitted by copyright law.

For permission requests, write to the publisher at the address below.

Yorkshire Publishing
3207 South Norwood Avenue
Tulsa, Oklahoma 74135
www.YorkshirePublishing.com
918.394.2665

Dedication

The Author and Cindy

This book of my memories is dedicated to my family and friends in Newport, especially my sister Cindy Johnston Sweat, who has had to hear these stories over and over and correct my mistakes. Post WWII babies were abundant in Newport in the late '40's and '50's. We were all so lucky to have a sibling or two near our age. Cindy and I still have adventures on our Girls Weekend Out trips and pass on our childhood escapades to the next generation. Special thanks to photographers Cheryl Mauldin and Delana Epperson for use of their photos and to Jamie Darling of Darling's Fine Things for hosting book events and continuing to promote Newport, Jackson County and the Arkansas Delta. In my childhood, Newport was pretty near heaven, and I'm proud to call it my hometown. I also cherish my friendships in the NHS Class of 1966.

New Kid on the 800 Block of McLain Street

My House in 1953 at 805 McLain Street

I grew up in a place where 'playing' became an art form. Summer in the 1950's in eastern Arkansas meant mosquitoes, chiggers, fireflies, and just plain fun. Wearing insect repellent in the summer was equal to putting on perfume in the winter. The pesky mosquitoes, so numerous because of the rice fields in the nearby river bottoms, came out in swarms as soon as the sun went down. I will never understand how we escaped cancer from riding our bicycles down the streets behind the mosquito fogger trucks each night.

Next Door Neighbors Lynn Alice and Jeff Jeffery with Me and Cindy

Good clean fun was abundant and second nature to most kids back then. We all piled into someone's mom's station wagon to go to the free movies on Saturday mornings at the Strand Theater downtown. We played outside till dark-thirty or the bugs drove us indoors. We slept with our windows wide open and prayed the peeping Tom did not make the rounds in our neighborhood that night. We had bicycles, tricycles, Mopeds, ping-pong tables, swing sets, hula-hoops, jacks, and roller skates to keep us busy all day through till dark if our parents didn't call us inside. Dogs weren't restrained and followed us everywhere we went and so did little sisters. I was the little sister this particular summer of 1953.

My 6th Birthday Cake

    That summer my family moved from Hortense Street near the city park to a new white frame house with an upstairs which was across the small lake that divided old Newport from the new section of the city unofficially called East Newport. In 1953 in East Newport, construction was going on everywhere. The streets of our new subdivision were just being paved and houses were in different stages of completion up and down McLain Street. When our block was finished, the sidewalks went from one end of the block to the other, perfect for skating and bike riding in my eyes. And there were alleys behind each row of houses so your garbage cans never had to be exposed for all to see.

    A favorite pastime during all the construction was drawing houses on the seldom-traveled side streets using leftover sheet rock as chalk. My friends and I would draw elaborate floor plans complete with furniture then sit in the so-called chairs we drew and 'play house.' All was well till a car or truck came down the street or the next rain washed our make-believe houses away. And I remember collecting everyone's discarded Christmas trees from the alley and making a Christmas tree lot in our back yard much to my dad's chagrin. Then the gang dug a tunnel in Paul Nichols' yard next door and his mom kept telling us to fill it up, but we put sticks over it, and his mom fell in it one day when she went out to hang clothes on the line. One summer we had a circus at Buddy Black's house on Holden. Fun times in the summertime. Never a dull moment.

Playing Cemetery before McLain Was Paved LtoR Jeff Jeffery, Mary Rachel Johnston, Gary Guthrie, Cindy Johnston, Paul Nichols

We liked to play 'cemetery' too. We would get an old 2" X 4" board and prop it up on both ends with saw horses. Each child would put a mound of mud or dirt on his/her 'grave' then decorate it with flowers and greenery picked from the neighbors' flowerbeds. Someone would be selected as the winner for having the best grave. Some parent made a picture of four of us with our sample graves one day. Then years later my sister Cindy was watching a Jonesboro television station and a picture of the four of us kids playing cemetery appeared on the screen.

It was part of a religious advertisement. The Reverend Cecil Guthrie's son Gary was one of the boys in the picture with Jeff Jeffery, my sister Cindy, Paul Nichols, and me; the Guthries had lived across McLain from us for several years. Rev. Guthrie, a Baptist minister, had used that photo in his weekly devotional on television. What memories flooded my brain when my sister called to tell me, as some of us were all grown and gone from McLain Street.

McLain Circa 1952

The Walnut Grove Cemetery was just three blocks behind McLain Street in East Newport, and in daylight hours we were allowed to go play there. In fact, my mother and Aunt Cathren McCartney took Cindy and I there many times to look over the resting places of relatives we had never known. There was Uncle Oscar, my mom's baby brother who had only lived six weeks and my grandfather Judge John Andrew Melville's big gravestone in the middle of the Melville plot. He died way before I was born. He had been county judge at one time and worked in the old Jackson County Court House at Jacksonport, which is now a state park. The Melville family plot (Melville was my mom's maiden name and she had lots of brothers and sisters) was large and stretched between two distinct cedar trees at the cemetery. I still visit the Melville plot each time I am in town. That cemetery is a place that holds many memories for me, not necessarily sad ones.

Lots of shade trees and green grass thick as carpet made the cemetery a nice place to play. I got my worst spanking for staying at the graveyard after dark. I was not staying after dark to scare someone as a joke either; I was just playing and reading the stones. Back in the 50's you just wandered around and played safely in your neighborhood until you heard your mom or dad calling your name in the evening air.

That evening I failed to hear, "Ma—ry, Ma—ry Rachel, it's time to come in!" So when I did show up under the street light one block down, it had become, "Mary Rachel Johnston, you get in this house right this instant! You are in a heap of trouble, young lady! I have been calling you for thirty minutes." I got very few memorable spankings growing up, but that was one of them.

My dad was part-owner of the local drug store where all the teenagers hung out around the soda fountain in the late 50's and 60's. It was only two blocks from McLain over to Malcolm Avenue where Headlee's Rexall Drug Store was located. It was open till ten at night so some summer evenings the McLain Street gang would walk over to have a soda or shake. Our route to the drug store if not on a bike was cutting through back yards and across front lawns to make a quick trip there. A path was actually worn in all those yards because we walked it so much. But no neighbors ever complained.

McLain Street Gang

One summer when we were kids Jeff Jeffery and I, and his cousin Tommy from out of town, had an ice cream soda drinking/eating contest at the drug store. I was ordering strawberry sodas that were made from vanilla ice cream scoops dropped into carbonated water with fruit flavoring added to produce a rich, foamy fizz that overflowed the top of the glass. You were given a straw and an ice teaspoon. These were yummy, and they cost more than the nickel or dime Coca Colas we usually ordered. But I had the advantage on Jeff here, as I just had to say, "Charge it, please." I think he was paying twenty-five cents for each one he ordered. After the third one apiece we were nearly throwing up and decided to walk back home. I proclaimed myself winner.

I spent so much time at that soda fountain growing up that I started collecting Coca Cola memorabilia as an adult after college. It was everywhere in my house and basement and in my office and library at work. People would ask why the school library was decorated in Coca Cola items, and I would have to tell them that a lot of my special childhood memories surrounded growing up behind a drug store soda fountain. I sold my coke collection when I retired from public school teaching in 2013.

When kids got a little older but still were too young to drive, a favorite summer pastime was ambulance chasing. We would have to ride bikes all across town or talk some one's older sister like Lynn Alice Jeffery or one of the Nuckolls' girls into taking us to see where the sirens were going. Newport was so small you just had to follow the sounds to locate the excitement, which might be a house fire, car wreck, or other accident. Our little world in the 1950's didn't seem to have robberies or murders as standard, daily occurrences. In fact, all of Newport was safe for the kids back then.

Rachel Shankles

Today my children are grown. But I still take my daughters and grands back to Newport often. We drive by the old drug store and turn from Malcolm towards Holden Avenue at the corner where Palmer's Gulf Station used to be. Then we turn onto left onto Mclain the old street and drive up the only hill in Newport. We are on that corner of McLain where Stanley Montgomery lived in the big red brick house, and the kids' heads turn to see the house where Nana and Aunt Cindy grew up. Dorcas and Jerry Jeffery resided in the red brick ranch-style house next door till their deaths then Lynn Alice lived there many years. Gary Guthrie's brick house is still across the street, but the Nuckols girls and other families lived there over the years. Our white clapboard house seems to look the same. Now my sister Cindy owns it as our mom and dad have moved on to rest at Walnut Grove just a few blocks away. Strike out I always have to go by there too. Walnut Grove Cemetery hasn't changed much except the cedar trees around the Melville plot have been cut down or blown down by storms. Now some times I have a hard time finding the Melville plot.

The kids on the block have grown up and moved on to become fine, hard-working citizens. No crooks in the bunch. I guess Cindy and Stanley of the neighborhood kids stayed in Newport all these years. I often wonder if Gary and Stanley and Jeff and Cindy and Kay have all these wonderful memories of McLain Street that I do. It was pretty close to heaven to me in 1953.

McLain Street Gang

Walnut Grove Cemetery

Strand Theater Where We Saw Free Movies on Saturday Mornings

East Newport School

East Newport School

My first memories of school days in Newport were in the fall of 1953 when my sister Cindy, who is just 14 months older than me, began first grade. We lived on McLain Street in East Newport and concrete sidewalks lined most of the four blocks down McLain from our house to the front steps of East Newport School. My trusty tricycle was my means of travel and travel I did.

Jeff Jeffery, Gary Guthrie, Stanley Montgomery, Paul Nichols, and my big sister Cindy were all in first grade that year at the huge red brick schoolhouse that was surrounded by huge persimmon trees. It was located right where the hospital is today. When all these guys left each morning for a long day of drudgery at school, my mom would visit one of the lady neighbors to enjoy coffee and chit chat between eight and nine o'clock in the morning. I got to tag along. Back then most mothers didn't work, you know. If mom and I went to Jeff or Paul's house, I got to play with all their toys. Can you imagine? I was in hog heaven touching all those things they would kill me for looking at any other time!

The big first graders thought they were big shots because they were already in school. I got them back by playing with their toys while my mom shared coffee and conversation with their mothers each morning. I did get lonely, but it was a wonderful life!

After coffee, mom and I headed home down the sidewalk; no need for a second automobile when walking was so convenient. Ten o'clock straight up meant a 'pause for refreshment.' In other words, Coca Cola time for mom. She had a cold, bottled coke every day of her life that I can remember at ten o'clock sharp. We kept cokes in wooden cases sitting on our back porch and refrigerated a few at a time for her morning ritual.

Author's Parents Peel and Rachel Johnston

After lunch and a nap, I hit the sidewalk on my tricycle and dashed towards the corner of McLain and Magnolia. I peddled in front of the Jeffery's house then down the hill in front of the Rogers' house (Dorcus Jeffery and Dottie Rogers were twin sisters) to wait by the stop sign under the shade of the big magnolia tree near the corner. And there I sat to await the return of those 'big kids' from school. And those first graders—Jeff, Gary, Paul, Stanley, and my sister thought they ruled the world. I'd be waiting for them expectantly after having to play alone all day, then boom! They blasted by me. They just pushed my tricycle out of the way and practically ran over me when they passed. Then they would call me 'baby' and hurt my feelings.

Me and My Beloved Tricycle

Cindy, Jeff, Kay Rhodes and the Author

Those boys hated my tricycle for some unknown reason. A few times they even took it away from me and sold it to kids on a nearby street. My poor dad had to go buy it back several times. I was very attached to it and even rode it to school a lot my first-grade year. I think now they were trying to make me 'grow up' by making fun of my ride.

My first-grade year got off to a bad start. I had had so much fun playing with everyone's toys when they were not home that I really did not relish the thought of beginning first grade in the fall of 1954. Besides, my sister had had Mrs. Holt and had told her teacher that in order for her little sister to start school the next year our family would have to paint shoes on my feet. Well, that was embarrassing to me and quite a shock to my parents when the social worker stopped by to check on our need for government assistance. My dad was a druggist and manager of a drug store just three blocks from our house and the school. It was an embarrassing situation.

McLain Street Gang

If that did not serve to damper my educational desires, the stories that everyone told about Mrs. McAuley sure did. I had heard she would pull your tongue out and slap it with a ruler or hit your fingers with a one. I was just not ready for that type of fear factor just yet. I did know one of the teachers though and I liked her a lot. My Aunt Cathren McCartney had taught first grade at East Newport for many, many years, but they told me I could not be in her room since she was my aunt. Cindy had not been allowed to be in her class the year before so she told me every day they would never let 'me' be in Aunt Cat's class either.

So, when school started in 1954, my dad drove the gang (some of the neighborhood boys and Cindy) to school the first few days on his way to work at the drug store. East Newport School housed first, second, and third grades. Dad drove a black two-door Ford coupe that year, and he would lean up over the steering wheel and flip that back seat up on his back to let all the kids out of the back seat right in front of the school.

The front of the brick building was lined with beautiful big persimmon trees, green bushes, bicycle racks, and concrete stairs up to the main floor where first grade was housed. The side yards had more persimmon trees and very tall slides and monkey bars and big swing sets. You could see the black metal fire escape zigzagging down the left side of the building. A cavernous cafeteria was in the basement (where all the students were lined up single file and given polio vaccine shots ever so often then sent out the back door to the playground if they didn't puke or faint or bawl their heads off) and the auditorium was between the first and second floors. (Oh, that auditorium, where we had the Tom Thumb Wedding in second grade with Lynn Dixon and Carolyn Wallis getting married!) And we made persimmon goulash in the huge roots of those giant trees at recess.

That first day of school in 1954 had a very high anxiety factor for me. When Dad stopped to let out the neighborhood kids and flipped up that seat, I never got out. I hid behind that high car seat in the floorboard. I ended up parked behind the drug store a few minutes later. There I got out and walked the three blocks home cutting through Palmer's Gulf Station to Holden and walking a block then going through Stanley's back yard to get back to McLain to my house—home sweet home. My mom didn't know what to do, but she thought I must be sick so she kept me home all day.

Author in Jeffery's yard

Day two of first-grade, I made the ride with the others down McLain to East Newport School again and got out with the other kids when my dad leaned up his seat, then I ran around to the other side and got right back in the back seat and hid before he had a chance to notice it. Same story second verse. The third day when dad made sure I was still standing there outside the car when he drove off, I was still determined not to go inside. I was petrified because I had Mrs. McCauley who whipped your tongue!!! I waited a little while and walked the four blocks back down McLain Street home.

Now my parents had to call the school for a pow-wow to find out just how they were going to get me to want to go to school. I told them that if I had Aunt Cathren for my teacher, I would go. They got the Principal Mary Nance to agree. I was a determined little brat, I guess. Best year of my school career! I had five pressed and starched dresses, one to wear each day.

Aunt Cathren McCartney

My Aunt Cathren was the best teacher in the world. Her room with those tall glass windows had a big wooden table in the center, big enough to have standing around space for every kid in the class. The table was piled high with all kinds of little toys of every color and description. Many a rainy day saw all her first graders playing around that table. There was always

Rachel Shankles

laughter in her room too, so I wasn't scared of being whipped or slapped with a ruler or paddle. My Aunt Cathren could get so tickled some times that I thought she was going to wet her pants or pass out. I had the most extraordinary first-grade year with her as my teacher. It set the stage for me to always love school and prefer to be there and not at home any more.

It stirred something in me that year that I haven't quite given up yet. I think it prepared me to become a life-long, dedicated teacher. You see, I taught public school myself for 42 years, and now I teach online graduate classes at the University of Central Arkansas.

Teaching is in my blood. Besides my Aunt Cathren McCartney, my oldest sister Sue Ann Smith taught second grade in Newport at the donut school (Gibb Castleberry) and my youngest daughter Amy Hutto is a teacher and school librarian at SouthSide Bee Branch near Damascus, AR. The Melville girls, my mother's five sisters lived all over Jackson County and were either teachers or nurses. My older daughter Nan Brand Means is a Nurse Practitioner. I love school. I love school buildings. I love libraries and books and writing. School is an adventure every day.

Sometimes these days my mind wanders back to East Newport School and the smell of the oiled floors and the fear of the cloak closets in the hall and the polio shots.

My own school classroom always had a non-threatening atmosphere so those scared or shy big kids wouldn't bolt and run back home. You see, I know how they feel that first day of school!

Author's Daughters Nan and Amy

The Author at school

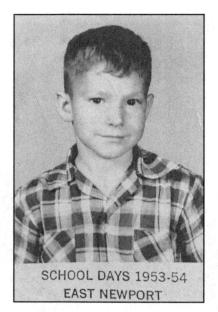

Jeff Jeffery

Me in First Grade

Small Town View of 1955

Tom Thumb Wedding

Brownies Scout meeting at Umsted Memorial Methodist Church

Rachel Shankles

I was seven in the fall of 1955. Elvis was the biggest news I knew anything about. His songs were a lot different from Tennessee Ernie Ford and Pat Boone, who I was used to hearing on the radio and seeing on black and white television. Later that year the airwaves revealed the new sounds of rock and roll from Chuck Berry and others as Elvis's music caught fire. The news called it rock-a-billy music; I called it fantastic. That spring found me singing "Love Me Tender" to Patric Brosh at the spring festival on the big wooden stage of the East Newport School auditorium with all the second-grade class.

Our school had wooden floors that were oiled not waxed. It had a distinctive smell to it; that smell was everywhere. Everything was wooden there but the front steps. You walked up about ten concrete steps to enter the two-story building, and you were on the first floor where first grade classrooms were with Mrs. Holt, Mrs. McAuley and Mrs. McCartney. Mrs. Cathren McCartney was my first-grade teacher and she was also my aunt. It was hard not to call her Aunt Cathren. Cloakrooms lined the wall of the wide entrance hallway. At the back of the huge hallway, you could see a large stairwell going up about half a flight to the auditorium, which was between the 1st and 2nd story. On both sides at the bottom of this stairwell to the auditorium were steps leading down to the basement cafeteria. On the auditorium level, the stairs parted and began two sets of stairs on either side leading on up to the top floor where second and third grade classrooms were housed. Just like downstairs, the main hallway up there was huge with cloak rooms lining the sides, and on the end of the building facing McLain Street there was a small office for the principal of the school. Our Principal in 1954-55 was Mrs. Mary Nance, who also taught second grade.

Mrs. Mary Nance, Principal

Mrs. Nance was my second-grade teacher and a very good friend of my Aunt Cathren's. I was just sure Aunt Cathren had told her ahead of time to look out for her little niece Mary Rachel. I did not have the anxiety and dread over second grade like I had the year before. But when Mrs. Nance called the roll that first day I realized there would be a lot of competition for her attention. Every Mary I had ever met in Newport was in that classroom this particular year. There was Mary Jane Williams, Mary Kathryn Smith, and me— Mary Rachel Johnston. I guessed that it would be double names this year, and that I was doomed to the Southern middle-name-calling syndrome. Little did I know then that at the University of Arkansas in Fayetteville some eleven years later, I would end up living right across the hall from another Mary Johnston from somewhere else in Arkansas and would have to immediately change my name to Rachel for

Rachel Shankles

the rest of my life. That is— for everyone BUT those who knew me growing up in Newport. If I get a phone call and they start with 'Mary Rachel,' I know they are back-home friends.

Another coincidence was that all of these Mary's were related to other teachers in Newport Schools! But Mrs. Nance was a pro. She put our desks in a semi-circle with two rows and memorized our names immediately. She would have to step out of the classroom occasionally to visit her office if the phone rang or a teacher brought a student in to be punished. She was so sweet and kind and always smiling. I cannot imagine her giving any mean little boys licks, but I heard them next door. She did not even get mad when Thomas Walker left his book satchel, yes, I said a book satchel, in the aisle and short little Mrs. Nance tripped over it and almost broke her neck. She was always in a good mood and could just smile and make the kids do whatever she was asking. She just made it sound like it would be fun to do math or draw pictures or learn to write our names! And we did! Yes, we learned cursive in second grade.

All the rest of our years in Newport schools meant Cindy and I went by drug store after school for a snack. And in later years, if Elvis had released a new record, it meant begging Dad for a dollar and going next door to the record shop to buy the 45 RPM version of the hit and running home to play it on the record player.

The Author 2nd Grade

On the black and white television set my parents had bought, we could watch *Louisiana Hayride* on Saturday night or *The Honeymooners* with Jackie Gleason. My mom and aunt got hooked on *Gunsmoke* and *As the World Turns* episodes. No, the sheriff never hung his hat at Kitty's place; he never even came close in 1955. We would lie in the floor with our heads in our hands waiting untill ten o'clock when our dad would come home from work at the drug store. We always got to stay up later than the other kids we knew just to see him before bedtime and say goodnight. Sometimes one of us got to rub his feet or fetch his slippers for a Yankee dime. The ten o'clock news was only fifteen minutes long back then and one reporter read the news, the weather and the sports in that length of time. Then it was time to hit the hay.

Rachel Shankles

We had Brownie Scouts at Umsted Memorial Methodist Church one block from school one afternoon a week and we walked across McLain Street to get there each time. Second grade was memorable too because my little brother was born that year. I remember being at school and out on the monkey bars when my Aunt Cathren came out to find me at recess on April 12th, 1955. She said I had a new baby brother. We usually had to fly out the door to get dibs on a monkey bar for recess because there were only a few; but that day, I was so happy that I gave up my monkey bar and just walked around with a big smile on my face. John Peel Johnston was born with Down's Syndrone, but he was the happiest little boy in Newport and he still thinks he knows everyone there.

Second grade in 1955 was awesome. Rock and roll music and television were brand new. I was big enough to walk home alone after school. My name had changed to a good Southern double-name and I had a new baby brother! And life in my home town was wonderful.

Cindy, John Peel, and Mary Rachel

John Peel Johnston

John Peel Johnston

John and Mary Rachel circa 2016

Oh, No! Not Again!
These Girls Will Eat Anything!

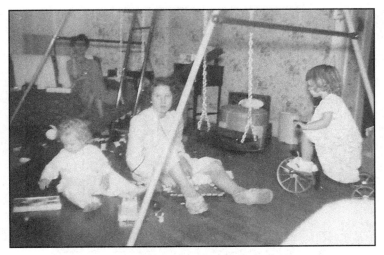

My sisters and I

My sister Cindy and I are barely a year a part in age. My mom always said she had her hands full when we were toddlers. I had a older half-sister too (Sue Ann Causey Smith), but it was mainly us little tikes that kept my mom and dad and the local doctors busy.

I always thought I was adopted. I always knew I was 'unplanned.' Maybe some of my thoughts grew out of the fact that my sisters tried to kill me right off the bat. When I was just a baby of maybe six months of age, my mom overheard one of my sisters saying, "Here, Mary, eat another one." She ran into the bedroom to find my siblings had me propped up on her bed and were feeding me something. When she was close enough to see what it was they were feeding me, she realized they weren't breath mints or M&M's but baby aspirin. "Here, Mary, eat another one." That was the first time my mom took me screaming to the emergency room to have my stomach pumped. And I don't even remember that time.

Cindy and I as Toddlers

Babies 14 months apart

McLain Street Gang

Cindy and I speak clearly now, but we must have been tongue-tied or something as little kids because we certainly had miscommunications with our parents at times. Our next-door neighbor Lynn Alice Jeffery invited us in her house one day when we were about 4 and 5 years old. Lynn Alice amazed us because she was our friend Jeff's big sister—a teenager. Lynn Alice gave us some candy that was delicious. Of course, we weren't supposed to be off at the neighbor's eating candy, and we came home rather sick from stuffing ourselves. When mom asked what we had been eating, we admitted the hard, cruel fact that we had been eating 'mothballs' all afternoon. Another screeching trip to ER and this time we both got our stomachs pumped. The mothballs turned out to be 'malt balls—the old fashioned kind that were 'covered in chocolate.'

I shouldn't have taken it out on Lynne Alice's little brother who was really bigger than me, but he was the first neighborhood boy I fed dog food sandwiches to when I got my little play stove. I don't think those boys ever knew what I was putting in those sandwiches. They didn't ever ask.

When Cindy was about seven, she came running home from a neighbor's screaming that she had a bee up her nose. My mom sure was gullible; I overheard one of my aunts call mom 'high strung' and never figured that out till I experienced the trait myself. She raced to the hospital with the rest of us in tow to find out it was a 'bead' not a 'bee,' but to me, that was still an emergency!

I have to tell you about the last trip to ER when we thought Cindy was going to get her stomach pumped; it didn't work out as planned. We had gotten birthstone rings for Christmas when we were about 10 and 11 years old; they had been tied to the tree on pretty ribbons that year (we always had to get the same, identical things from Santa for some strange reason). About a week after the holiday we were walking around the neighborhood down by Debbie Albright's house towards the cemetery (that is a whole other story) to play. Cindy took off her ring and threw back her head and said, "I am going to catch this ring on that little hang-me-down thing at the back of my throat." So I watched as she held up the ring and dropped it into her upturned mouth. Kaplunk! The instant it hit her throat you know what happened—she swallowed it. We turned around and ran home as she moaned, "I can feel it stuck in my throat."

Again, a rushed visit to the doctor's office. The X-ray machine was somewhat of a novelty in those early days. Salenfriends, a local downtown Newport clothing and shoe store, had one in their store that X-rayed your feet to see how the shoes fit. The kids played with it sticking hands or feet in it to see their bones (who knew that was dangerous back then). All the way up there to the hospital this particular day, my mom would say, "Cindy, can you still feel it?"

Cindy and Mary in front of 805 McLain St.

McLain Street Gang

And Cindy would say, "Yes, and it hurts." But right as we walked into the doctor's office, she said, "Momma, it doesn't hurt anymore." That day the new X-ray machine showed a shiny ring at the bottom of her esophagus in her stomach. The doctor said it was too late to do anything. "This too shall pass," he told my mom. Cindy and I were at a loss as to what that meant.

My parents treated Cindy like a queen there for a while after this incident. I still don't know where she got that hair-brained idea. I think it was because she was always having tonsillitis and having doctors and nurses stare down her throat. She was just too conscious of that hang-me-down thing and wanted to see just what it could do. We were never given jewelry again.

Now jump to my own children's odd habits of eating weird stuff. My daughter Amy ate a slug in the yard when she was a toddler. I watched her playing with a Frisbee and saw something black on it that she picked up. As I ran off the porch knowing it would go straight to her mouth, I saw that it was a slug—a garden-variety snail. And. yes, it went straight into her mouth. Those are the slimiest creatures in the world. You know they leave a streak of slime wherever they crawl, and I was gagging trying to clean her mouth out. I could not imagine all that slime in her throat! I grabbed my skirt tail and started wiping out her mouth as I carried her in to wash it out.

Then my son Austin had this odd fascination with dog water when he was just a toddler. Dog water. You know, the kind in rusted tin cans that sit in the back yard with old, stagnant water for the outdoor dogs to drink. Every time I let him out in the yard and turned my back, Austin had that old tin can turned up drinking it. So, being the good mother, I called the pediatrician and said I was sure this child had some kind of vitamin deficiency to cause him to crave that rusty old dirty water all the time. "No," he said, "don't worry about it."

Rachel Shankles

Well, worry I did, because pretty soon he was not only drinking the dog's water but eating the dog's food every single day. So, being the good mother, I called the doctor again. At least I wasn't running to the ER as much as my mother had with me. The doctor said again, "No, problem; it won't hurt him."

I knew something had to be wrong because pretty soon I looked out and he was literally biting the dog as hard as he could. The sweet collie just stood there as Austin grabbed a hunk of fur and laid his teeth into it—hot, sweaty, uncombed collie fur. Yuk! I knew something medically had to be wrong with this child (he later got kicked out of several babysitters for biting—it should have been a forewarning of that). I called the doctor ONE MORE TIME to explain and ask for help because I just knew it was a vitamin deficiency (where I got that I do not know to this day). The baby doctor solemnly said, "Lady, don't call me back till he starts barking." Click. I never took any of my children back to that pediatrician after that.

So I know what it's like to have two in diapers, two toddlers running around and into everything with a somewhat jealous big sister.

Author's children Nan, Amy, and Austin circa 1980

Cindy and Mary today

Headlee's Rexall Drug Store

Headlee's Storefront

Peel Johnston, the author's dad

Rachel Shankles

My dad Peel Austin Johnston began working in a drug store on Front Street in downtown Newport as a teenager, sweeping up and working as a soda jerk. After graduating from Newport High School and having several odd jobs (like privy inspector), he went to the Army and became a Medic during WWII. After coming back, he trained first, I think, with Jimmy Shannon in his store down town. Then worked as druggist for Brown's Drug Store at Front and Walnut downtown which was purchased by Frank Headlee of Searcy. It then became Headlee's Rexall Drug Store.

There were many drug stores in Newport back then—Shannon-Ritter Drug Store, Brown's Drug Store and Grimes' Drug Store all on Front Street in Newport.

Dad was a licensed druggist and took lengthy tests at the state Capitol to obtain that licensure when pharmacy degrees became required. He eventually bought part ownership in Headlee's Drug Store, Inc., with the Headlee family from Searcy (where another Headlee's Drug Store was located). The store moved to East Newport on Malcolm a few years before we moved from Hortense Street to McLain Street in about 1953, I think. It expanded every few years in the late 50's and early 60's taking in the record shop next door at one time.

Before Newport had Walmart, the drug store was the place to buy toys for Christmas and birthdays and Russell Stover candy for Valentine's Day. I still have an original Barbie from the store. Headlee's on Malcolm had the soda fountain where all the teens hung out. My mom's friends met for coffee at 4 o'clock every day of the week forever. It is where many of you learned to say "Charge it!" I remember the red booths, the bar stools that swiveled, cokes for a nickel or a dime, and the juke box.

I went to the drug store for breakfast, lunch and before dinner and after supper, either by foot or bicycle hundreds of times, daylight or dark. I had saddlebag baskets on the back of my bicycle and road my brother John Peel along with me most times.

McLain Street Gang

The author's dad working

Cindy working as soda jerk

After a ballgame at Headlee's

I lovingly remember all the beautiful ladies who worked at the front counter of the drug store selling everything from cosmetics to comic books and candy. They were the mothers of my friends like Imogene Rawlings, mother of Rayma and Pam, Linda Treadway's mom Mildrene Barker, Bea Knopp, Jeanne Wilson Moore's mom Midge Wilson, and Mrs. Jan Ivy. Elbert Bridgeman and Gaylon Dilday were other pharmacists there a long time, and Jimmy Darling began working there early in his career. Jessie Curry was the delivery boy for many years, and I learned to drive in his delivery van that had a stick shift. He took me to school and picked me up after school if I couldn't get a ride home with Dorcus Jeffery.

When the new Harris Hospital was built in East Newport, the Headlee corporation added a smaller Headlee's store katy-cornered from it, but it only remained there two or three years. My dad retired and sold his shares in Headlee's in the 1970's

McLain Street Gang

then the store closed a few more years later. Jimmy probably knows the exact year.

Most people thought my dad's nickname was "Mr. Pill", but his real name was 'Peel'. I sure spent hours of my childhood in that store, and I began working behind the soda fountain in seventh grade during summers and school holidays. There is a rumor I got fired for spending too much time flirting with boys while sitting on the ice cream boxes. I do remember getting chewed out by Dad for forgetting to put cheese on cheeseburgers and bananas in banana splits. But actually, I just got promoted to the front.

I visited the old drug store building last time I was in town as it is now the Old Treasures resale shop for my brother's special school Arkansas Center for Independence. It looks great inside.

But it is missing the soda fountain and Crews and Lindsey's Grocery Store on the right side and Angela's Dress Shop on the left...Such fond memories I have of growing up in a small town.

Front Porch Memories on Laurel Street

Nonna by Her Front Porch

My grandmother, Bess Holmes Jones, lived in the old part of Newport, Arkansas, not far from the downtown area on Laurel Street. She had a modest white frame house with a screened-in porch and carport added in the early 1960's. It is the early sixties memories from that porch that flood my mind

Rachel Shankles

any time I'm back in my hometown and turn down that once tree-lined street where the Duncan girls grew up.

That little front porch was occupied every day in spring and summer by my grandmother and her visitors. It was truly a Southern luxury to sit and sip iced tea or lemonade as you rode back and forth on the cushioned glider, which of course was reserved for visitors. Nonna, as we called our father's mother, had her favorite green and white metal chair that was always full of chintz-covered pillows, and there was a ceiling fan going and sometimes a radio playing from a small table if a ballgame was being broadcast from St. Louis.

The streets of that area of Newport were all lined with concrete sidewalks and tall old oak trees. All the sidewalks led towards downtown. Although Newport was not built on a square like a lot of Southern cities, downtown Newport had a main street with stores that stayed open till late on Saturday nights. You could smell those Front Street popcorn vendors from Nonna's porch all day on Saturdays. That's when the farmers would come to town to buy groceries, you know.

Sitting on Nonna's porch on a Saturday, you would see a constant stream of folks making their way on foot into town. Everyone was friendly and many were often heard saying, "Good evening" or "Hello, Mrs. Bess!" And many were asked to come in to sit a spell before they had to move on to attend to their business. This parade of people went on all day on Saturdays, and I hated to have to leave the porch to go in for meals when all of society seemed to be walking across the front yard. The front porch was definitely the place to be on this day of the week, and I loved to spend Saturdays with my grandmother.

That porch was so peaceful and relaxing. Some times when I was younger, Nonna would rock me in that glider and gently rub my back or my face. It was heaven on earth. I would sometimes rub her soft hands as we glided. My dreams were

McLain Street Gang

often interrupted with "Howdys" and "Good afternoon's" from strangers walking by the little porch, which was maybe 12 feet from the sidewalk.

In my late twenties, I wrote a poem about my grandmother's soft, silky hands, and it was published by the *Arkansas Democrat* in the Sunday issue that used to contain a Poetry Column. Nonna was not impressed when she saw that poem dedicated to her, as she had always thought she had ugly hands. I thought they were angel's hands—purple veins and all! Do all little girls think their grandma's are angels?

I think my favorite memory of that porch was in 1966 when I was a high school senior and could drive. One morning in earl spring I stopped by grandmother's before school for some strange reason. She was finished with breakfast already as it was maybe 7:30 AM so we sat on her porch for a while and rocked before I went to school. Sure enough, there came a steady stream of folks walking to work in the downtown area. "Good morning! Looks like a nice day, doesn't it?" And some stopped by to chat a spell before moving on to work. I was absolutely fascinated by that early morning ritual. I had thought it was purely a Saturday thing! It let me know there was a whole other working world out there.

In my opinion, a front porch in the South can be a little piece of heaven on earth. Many a memory originates there. My grandmother's porch is still there but enclosed at the little white house on Laurel Street, but she went on to heaven in 1991 at the age of 97.

She really disliked this poem I had published in the *Democrat* when she was 88:

Rachel Shankles

GRANDMA

Why are grandmother's hands so warm?
And their purple veined skin so soft?
I think it's from all the hugging, holding,
caring and sharing they do.
I'll always remember holding my grandma's warm,
Silky hand on shopping trips
Even when I was a very big girl,
Too big to hold girls' hands anymore.
But it never bothered me;
It made me feel proud to let her know
That I'd be strong and carry on when she was gone.
Those same warm, silky hands that taught me how to pray
Go on hugging, holding, caring and sharing...
Even now at 88.

As I look at the faded copy of that newspaper, I think it must have been the clipart they added of a very old lady that she really disliked.

Now my hands look just like hers!

Mrs. Bess Holmes Jones, My Nonna

The White River Bridge at Newport

The Blue Bridge Courtesy of Cheryl Mauldin

The White River Bridge at Newport, affectionately now called 'The Blue Bridge,' will soon be torn down. I hate that. It holds special memories for me, my children, and my 1966 NHS classmates. Not only did I swim and play below that bridge growing up, but traveling anywhere but Jonesboro, Memphis or St. Louis required crossing that bridge.

The Bridge from the South

We crossed that bridge to visit my grandfather A.L. Johnston, who had a grocery store at Russell and a strawberry farm out in the hills above Russell. I had aunts, uncles and cousins to visit in Little Rock and made many a trip to Fayetteville and back after graduating from NHS. We learned to swim in that river at the Cut Off and my family always had a boat on the river. I crossed that bridge so many times, and it sure caused more excitement coming back home than leaving.

I remember my dad chasing a school bus out Hwy 67 over the bridge half way to Bradford one Saturday when I was in junior high when he accidentally overslept and Linda Barker, my best friend (who spent many a night at my house,) and I missed the early morning bus for a scheduled trip to Little Rock to the

McLain Street Gang

Home Economics Convention which was always a big deal. We would dress in our Easter finest and roam downtown Little Rock and have meetings at Robinson Auditorium in the spring each year. But the bus left at like 7AM. My dad had planned to wake us up and take us out to eat breakfast before boarding the bus, but he overslept, which was so out of character for him. He woke up late and got us downstairs and had us dress in the car on the road as he sped over that bridge to catch that Newport School District bus. And we did catch it, pulling alongside and honking like crazy till the driver pulled over. Whew!

I lived in North Little Rock four years and taught English at Sylvan Hills High School. Then I moved to Hot Springs and taught school at Lakeside High School for 38 years. My 3 kids were raised in Hot Springs, and we traveled to Newport a lot over their formative years. Good old Highway 67 was only two lanes. It has really changed over the years of my life.

Every time we approached that bridge, I would start slowing down. Pushing in and letting out on the gas pedal; the car would start sputtering. I would say, "Oh, no, we are about to run out of gas, kids!" Then more of the in and out on the gas pedal and as we approached the middle of the bridge, the car was almost at a standstill.

Three kids with eyes real big were hollering about what to do next. I would say, "Last one that screams has to walk!" and everyone hollered at once. What fun that always was no matter how many times we crossed that bridge into my old hometown.

I graduated from Newport High School in 1966. My 50th reunion of the Newport Class of 1966 was the summer of 2016 so we arranged to go to Front Street and have one last photo made of us and the Blue Bridge during our Saturday visit to Newport. It really has sentimental value to all the guys and gals in my class. The beach under the bridge was active during our high school years. Many paintings and photos have been made of that old bridge, but soon a new modern one will span the White River at Newport.

Still today when Nan or Amy and their kids ride with me to Newport, they ask to take Old Highway 67 to go over that old blue bridge. And you can bet someone will say,

"I think we are running out of gas…last one to scream has to walk!" Then screams ensue.

Great memories of my home town Newport, Arkansas.

Class of '66 in 2016 by the Bridge

The Bridge at Nightfall Courtesy Delana Epperson

CPSIA information can be obtained
at www.ICGtesting.com
Printed in the USA
BVHW04s2342051018
529422BV00010B/60/P